THE DANGEROUS SHIRT

BOOKS BY ALBERTO RÍOS

POETRY

The Dangerous Shirt

The Theater of Night

The Smallest Muscle in the Human Body

Teodoro Luna's Two Kisses

The Lime Orchard Woman

Five Indiscretions

Whispering to Fool the Wind

FICTION

The Curtain of Trees

Pig Cookies

The Iguana Killer

MEMOIR

Capirotada

LIMITED EDITIONS

The Warrington Poems

Sleeping on Fists

Elk Heads on the Wall

THE DANGEROUS SHIRT

ALBERTO RÍOS

COPPER CANYON PRESS

PORT TOWNSEND, WASHINGTON

Printed in the United States of America

Cover art: Fernando Botero, *Hombre con perro*, 1989. Oil on cloth, 129.5 x 104 cm. Museo Botero, Bogotá. Collection Banco de la República de Colombia.

Copper Canyon Press is in residence at Fort Worden State Park in Port Townsend, Washington, under the auspices of Centrum. Centrum is a gathering place for artists and creative thinkers from around the world, students of all ages and backgrounds, and audiences seeking extraordinary cultural enrichment.

LIBRARY OF CONGRESS CATALOGING-IN-PUBLICATION DATA

Ríos, Alberto.
 The dangerous shirt / Alberto Ríos.
    p. cm.
  ISBN 978-1-55659-298-0 (alk. paper)
  I. Title.

PS3568.I587D36 2009
811'.54—dc22

                                        2008046600

COPPER CANYON PRESS
Post Office Box 271
Port Townsend, Washington 98368
www.coppercanyonpress.org

ACKNOWLEDGMENTS

These poems appeared in earlier versions in the following journals:

Alaska Quarterly Review, Arizona Highways, Burnside Review, Cimarron Review, Columbia Poetry Review, The Fiddlehead, Fifth Wednesday Journal, Indiana Review, Knockout, Narrative, Ploughshares, Poet Lore, Poetry East, Prairie Schooner, The Quirk, Rio Grande Review, Runes, Smartish Pace, The Virginia Quarterly Review, and *Willow Springs.*

"The Rain That Falls Here," originally published in *The Virginia Quarterly Review,* was included in *The Best American Poetry 2008,* edited by Charles Wright.

For Lupita.
A very happy thirtieth anniversary.

CONTENTS

THREE

We spend our lives imagining otherwise.

FOUR

I will do what I can.

THE DANGEROUS SHIRT

ONE

I stand on the invisible floor of the night.

TUESDAY SOUP

In Monday's soup, you put in
What you have—

Leftovers from Sunday,
Chicken, red rice, cilantro.

On Tuesday, you put in
What you have

Even less of now,
The one leftover piece of dark chicken

Nobody wanted, the suspect
Rice with the black-rim

Stain from something, something
That got dropped, or from a spoon

Dipped into something else first
Then used in the rice, a stain

Growing darker by the hour,
Darker and bigger.

On Tuesday, dinner skates
At the edge of the ice.

Wednesday is something safe,
Starting over with fresh beans,

A trip to the grocery store, *jícama*,
Bananas and chilies, all fresh, all new.

Thursday survives by luck,
Living on the enthusiasms of Wednesday,

The small piece of pork that was on sale,
The other extras, the olives,

The big sack of soft avocados
Too ripe to wait, which is why they were so cheap.

Friday begins the weekend,
Three days that take care of themselves in the world.

But Tuesday, Tuesday is what people remember,
Like it or not, Tuesday, so easy to forget

Otherwise. Tuesday, always circumstance and luck,
A day in which gamblers sit at the dinner table,

Unfortunate and miserable. But in the quiet attempt
Whoever cooks dinner makes,

Tuesday is the day
All great discoveries are made.

ON THE BUMPERS OF THE FORDS
IN THE LOT

1

High-school fights were the worst,
Young boys losing their teeth

Against the chrome fenders of cars,
Boys as they got thrown and then flew

Then hit
One kind of ground or another.

There was always a second of nothing
As the world came back to the boy,

As the tooth loosed itself out,
As the blood rubbed on a shirtsleeve

Made of itself a half-inch red flag.
The fallen boy would always be angry

Instead of sad. The other boy would always be shouting
Come on instead of *Go away. Go away.*

2

Or *Stop*.
The winner would be only half-standing himself.

The boys, the boys all went off to their lives.
From these two fighting, and two more,

From the hundred fights before and after,
The chrome on all their cars took a red to it,

Another red, as even before this
So many animals had given themselves to it,

Flies and gnats, moths, June bugs, dogs,
Cats and rabbits, sometimes deer—

All of them, too, making a raised mosaic of fluids
Hardened into something else on the shine,

Something half red and half green, yellow, half
Animal, half something from the mouth of a boy.

3

Much of this blood got lost in the carwashes
Through the months, but not all of it.

The years finally dulled the chrome anyway,
But a few spots would not go. They turned

Black, and spread out like small leaves.
No matter what, some of the bits held on this way,

Dark fossils, hard ferns in soft steel,
Beyond science and explanation:

They stayed not as things but as memory,
Moments that would be forgotten by the boys

But not by the things they hit or fell against,
Not by a world still stopped in that moment.

This was the last of the boys in their heat:
Blood on chrome, chrome turned black.

FALL AGAIN

Today brings an old news:
The brown and ocher, yellow colors of fall, of falling

Leaves and bark, the dark
Itself falling sooner, and soon again

Complaints about how cold the mornings are,
The old, certain song of the centuries sung

By us but by the world outside as well, sung
In the sound of the single bird

Leaning hard on the fence against
The season's first wind, wind the worst

Part of the new kind of day fall brings,
This late season, this low sun.

The call of things-to-do speeds me
Through this world, this changed world.

2

A broken strand of web spins in the air
As I walk by a garden wall. It spins in the air

Coaxed by the small wind, the gust I make
Passing by. I walk on the ground but see

No ground beneath me—canoe-shaped leaves,
Small and thousands and curled in on themselves,

They pretend they are the ground and the world.
They send a noise as I step on them, a voice, but so many

Speaking at once, I cannot make out the words,
The garbled din of it all, nothing I haven't heard before,

Though in all that hearing I hear only noise, nothing more.
The soft crunch, the soft next step as well, more voices,

More noise, and grackle birds, and cars hunching by.
As a car passes, a strand of my own hair wisps out.

IN AN EXCHANGE TWO BOYS MAKE

I saw the bear and nothing else. I cannot remember
My half of the bargain, what I offered

For the toy, a cast-iron marvel that was heavy in hand.
I cannot remember what I offered, what could be offered

Equal in some way to this thing that was perfect
In that weight, in that way it mattered in my hand.

I gave him a horse, but I don't know what else
I must have offered as well.

The horse I was trading was hobbled
Where the bear was fierce in its hunched lumbering.

The horse I was trading was worn
Where the bear, too, was worn, but on the bear

The meager paint was a sign of that beast's
Being bigger than the brown paint that tried to hold it.

I FELL TO THE FLOOR, AND KEPT ON

1

I fell to the floor and kept falling.
The shore of the ground

Stopped me, at first,
The way I expected,

The way the world expects, the way
It had stopped me every time before this.

But pure mathematics, pure chance,
This one time, this single time,

Perhaps ever in the history of the world
But having always been possible,

This one time, something happened:
Something happened in all the broken parts of me,

All the separate things that combined to be me,
The trillion trillion cells.

2

I could not with my eyes see those cells as broken apart,
But they were in some loose confederation

That made me, some uneasy cells
Holding hands with each other for now.

This time they spilled through and around and in a heat past
The trillion separate barriers of the ground,

The ground's cells themselves holding hands only loosely,
All of this a game of Red Rover, all these cells

Mimicking those Fifties movies of so many people
Going through turnstiles to get onto the subway,

These trillion cells and these trillion barriers
This one time moving easily and quickly by each other,

Each with its golden ticket, with no need for security,
Each one smiling, each on its way, everything moving.

3

They passed by each other like water through a grate
In some perverse version of *Have a Nice Day,*

Each moving in orderly, if rushed, fashion,
Having paid attention during all those fire drills,

All those things they said: *Be calm, leave your stuff.*
We—all the parts of me and All the Parts of the Ground,

We were matched in our minute mismatch.
I went through and past and by and around and onward

With nothing to stop me and me polite enough
Not to stop anything going in the other direction,

Going up, busily going up as I was busily falling,
But falling made new as stepping through the ground

Into the outer space of the deep underneath,
Into the vast frontier of the spaces-in-between.

4

I stepped into what had only seemed like darkness, like hardness.
It was as if I had walked into a movie theater,

Dark already the moment before the movie starts.
I could not see left or right.

It was a big darkness, wide and deep and high,
An elephant black, a whale black,

Loam- and oil- and obsidian-colored black.
I felt as if I were falling instead of sitting,

As if the movie theater seat were suddenly adrift
In a vast water.

I recognized this place as dream ground.
I had stood on it before, standing and not standing.

Here, the sky was full of anti-stars, of also-stars,
Quartz and glass buttons, tin lids and dimes.

5

Mirror shards and cellophane seen at a distance—
If this were a dream, all these things combined into what might be stars.

But they might be stars, the stars of this new place.
These were the stray things that had fallen into the ground

Before me, but in the same way I had, fallen
The way things fall through a sewer grate

Far enough that they can't be reached, traveling
By chance, out of hand, too fast, beyond reflcx.

And this might be a dream. But it is not a dream
In that I push off something black,

Something my hands see, push off hard and backward,
My good fortune holding—

The same way I fell in, I force myself back out,
The polite passing and exchange of cells, luckily, still at work.

6

I am—just as quickly as it happened—back on my knees in the kitchen,
My hands firm now on the ground of the floor

As they have been ten thousand times before.
I get up and dust myself off, shake my head.

When I fell, gravity called where space did not—
Space, Up, had never been a friend.

But falling was easy, comfortable, falling
Toward it, whatever it was, gravity

That great voice, those big hands
Waving me in. It was no work or trouble at all.

I am uneasy, now, and slower in my walk these days.
I trip easily still

As sometimes I step into the ground
Now that I know the way.

I SAW YOU TOMORROW

You're on an airplane
In a car. You're in a car

On the bus. You're on the bus
Going home as you daydream

At your desk. On your desk
You have a postcard of Alaska.

You are never where you are,
And when you are, you're leaving,

Late already for something else,
A meeting, a class, shopping,

And isn't shopping fun, you think,
Like being on a sightseeing tour.

But you're late and must get home,
Or you're home and must get going,

Late either way, exasperated,
Tapping your foot to get us all

Out the door. Goodbye, you wave
To yourself, standing there.

THE DANGEROUS SHIRT

The shirt in my closet is dangerous.
I shouldn't have ironed it.

Because I have, I will put it on.
If I put it on, I will be dressed.

If I am dressed, I will be drawn toward the door,
The door and not the couch—the door,

Because if I am dressed,
I will not want to lie down.

I will not want to get wrinkled, spoiling,
After all, the hard work of ironing the shirt.

If I am dressed and standing at the door,
I will want to go out and I will go out—

Because what else can I do
If I can't lie on the couch?

So if I get near the door, that's it—
Shake your head for me, because I will open it.

And if I open it, I will go through it.
I will go through it and close it behind me.

The danger of the shirt—of course,
Always, every moment, it is so obvious.

THE INJURED THUMB

1

He hurt his thumb as he was cleaning
The fireplace, its grate

Falling unexpectedly
From where he had stood it

Against the inside brick of the wall.
He felt nothing at first,

Then the stiffness and the growing
Red feeling, red, red, red.

A little skin was roughed up but not much—
There wasn't enough to show anyone,

Not enough for a dressing or a Band-Aid.
The moment instead lived inside his thumb

And could not, beyond its one word, speak itself
Very well. Pressing another finger against

The thumb—it made the pain
More, and pressing more made even more,

As if he had discovered a pain factory,
Or a mine full of red gold and bruise silver.

He said little to anyone about what had happened—
I hurt my thumb. It hurts.

Friends did not stop in their tracks.
He flexed it for them, but there was little to see.

The story and the moment and the pain,
They were all his.

2

All right, I confess. The thumb was mine.
I said nothing because, what was there to say?

I hurt myself. You hurt yourself. Everybody
Hurts. It's always in season, I know.

Still, I wanted to champion the small pain,
But who listens to the one hurt?

Quieted after shouting, I watched myself
Pour coffee to the rim of a cup, to the fill of a sigh.

I watched the steam of it rise,
The liftings off the surface of its small ocean,

That incipient hurricane of mild delight.
The wisps of curl coming off the coffee

Formed around my thumb as I lifted the cup.
My thumb hurt, still. I tried to drink the coffee

But couldn't. The thumb and the wisp, however,
They found each other. They did not let go

So easily. I put the coffee down
But the wisp followed. It disappeared

Around or into my thumb. That is,
I couldn't see it anymore. I thought at first

The throbbing was from having lifted the coffee,
But I could feel the wisp now,

Talking in a low voice to my thumb, inside it.
And I could feel my thumb answering back.

3

My thumb, that small pain I wouldn't listen to,
It left me for someone else.

To me, the moment was a half second
In which I felt, or did not feel, a numbness,

But that's all any of us needs. The thumb
And the wisp made a century of the half second.

The small nature of the event—the small
Nature of any event—will not be denied its large

Feeling, though it may seem only a moment to you.
As the thumb has taken pains to show me, however,

A moment is a moment and that moment is everything.
I, apparently, was not sympathetic enough.

Finding the century hidden inside every half second,
My thumb took its chance, to give

And take comfort, the thumb and the wisp
Together right there in the bed of my own hand.

I myself had not listened to the thumb. I had
Shaken my head, had shouted,

But for myself not for the thumb,
Which had, after all, taken the brunt of things.

And now, what to do? I've apologized, but to no good.
My thumb, even weeks later, now, will not do

The things I ask, and is loud, rude to me, even,
Carrying on and in love still, just to spite me.

A MAN WITH POCKETS

Putting something in his pockets began simply enough.
A young man: first it was a black comb.

A new brown wallet followed, his own house key,
Some spare change, a small knife—

The gift of an eighteenth birthday, the last way left
His parents could say, *Take care of yourself.*

These were not any longer the quartz and igneous rocks,
The green-backed, still-moving beetles,

The chewing gum prizes saved of childhood.
These were new pockets, bigger pants, and new ideas.

The things in his pockets grew up as he grew up.
The key soon enough imagined its need for a key chain,

And not simply something plain. Perhaps a companion key,
As well, the back shed's key, that grizzle-toothed brass finger.

The small knife, everyone agreed, would be elegant in a sheath,
A nice, three-color plastic-lace braid hanging from it.

2

The wallet set up an entire business of its own, quickly
Under its own management and with no board of directors:

It gathered cards for all manner of transaction and recognition,
Allowance and identification, direction and appointment.

It gathered photographs and coupons, paper money at last,
And everything else that might be prodded into folding.

The pockets looked like the cheeks of a chipmunk
And were big enough to give him the aspect of a pontoon boat.

On most days he began to walk more slowly,
But on windy days nobody could keep up with him.

He started to look for pants with more pockets,
Or rather, he *had* to look for them.

A handkerchief, which he never used, some balled-up tissues
He thought he would use but didn't use, either,

Sometimes a small book, or his lunch, a sandwich,
Some cookies, and some potato chips.

3

His new pockets filled just as quickly as the old ones.
He could never wear shorts.

And finally he could not sit.
He tried, but it was easier not to.

And then it was easier not to walk so much at all.
Instead, people came to him.

They came at first to offer consolation, to assure him
It was not unusual, this richness of circumstance, really.

But consolation was soon followed by reward,
Unexpected—a knife-sharpener, a new pair of socks,

All the things he had and which they needed.
And they were curious things, not things

Readily available anywhere else, not in stores,
Certainly. These were the things found in drawers,

Discarded at first, or saved for later,
Then suddenly and altogether necessary.

4

He could not walk but he gave flight to so many others,
A lightness of spirit at having found something

Irretrievably lost otherwise. He gave happiness
Where others had thought to give it to him.

This was the bargain, then, that he made with the world.
He would keep the small things at his side

In exchange for the big things not seeing him,
Not needing him, not paying him any attentions.

And it was a kind of life, free of tigers and danger,
But love, too, free of that and not entirely satisfying.

A bargain was a bargain, however, and his life was calm.
It was a full-enough life, a way to move, a way of breathing

Without moving. He became something else,
Not himself. A place, a garden, a store,

Everything but what he had been—a little boy
Believing in the necessary things of the world.

IN NIGHT

1

The light in the sky at night is old—and under those stars
We are illuminated by the billion years past,

Charmed, as we look up, by everything that has already happened
Somewhere in a time before all of us, and before that.

Night is a collective memory, not all of it ours.
The past is our tail, behind us. No matter what we do, it wags us

Quietly as we sit at its very end and reach of light.
The star shine is old, they tell us, light from many years past,

Centuries, light from beyond them, from a deep time,
From far away. This is the light that has come to us,

Mysterious, without introduction, without true name,
Light simply and easily and calmly always there.

2

Though who does not understand: it is so clearly a mother
Looking for her child, flashlight in hand, frantic.

We are looking at older light than our grandparents saw.
They were closer to when things happened out there in the dark.

What they saw was newer, fresher, brighter light, different light,
Light that still carried words with it, smells, feeling—

Something from the moment that made it. Perhaps
Our grandparents' stories about what they saw in their nights:

All of it was true. In stronger light, their ghosts, those people,
The things we cannot seem to see now,

They are not the mystery they seem, all those ghost stories
We were told and at which we laughed, and shook our heads.

3

Perhaps the ghosts themselves are science: And our proof
That they are nothing—this is the legend we ourselves have made up,

The story our grandparents cannot believe, no matter
How hard we try to convince them, saying *We do not see what you saw.*

In darkness, our own Saturday night story is what we call science now.
Its explanations, gleaned from dimmer light—no wonder

They make our grandparents shake their heads. But they saw.
They tell stories that we cannot—they remember

Who is related to whom, every last one. *How can you remember
All that?* we ask, all the family stories, places they used to live,

Things they used to do, dances. They saw their lives so clearly lit up,
That everything burned in as image, photographed inside them.

4

Everywhere we look, there are stars. Everywhere we look is backward
In time. Every direction. Everywhere we look is behind us.

Which way is forward? The past is in front of us. It comes at us
From all directions, as much from behind, in front, to the sides.

Above and below. To look forward, to see the future, should we
Look to our light? Should we look at the sun? Or beyond it?

We have been told not to look at the sun, which has kept us
From what it might be hiding. But that is old thinking.

Do not look at the sun because you will burn your eyes—
This is how it has always been. Everybody knows this.

It gives us the faith to predict that this is how it will always be. But,
What if it is an impediment to the direction in which we must look?

5

Night and the stars surround us. They surround the planet.
Night surrounds the sun as well, which tries every day

So hard to make us think otherwise, to make us think
That the day it makes, and gives us, is splendidly, brightly,

Everything. The reverse, after all, is unthinkable—that day
Is the blink of an eye, that day is darkness, is not seeing.

All well and good. The past is big, the present is now,
The future, it just shows up out of nowhere.

Still, here we are, you and I, not thinking any of this, and better off.
Nana saw a ghost. It was her father. We laugh.

It is ourselves we want to be now, rather than that other story,
The story that says ours is a dim, slight porch light in the vastness.

ACROSS THIS BRIDGE OF DREAMS

1

A river of buried tigers
Under a smooth bridge of undisturbed dreams.

Close your eyes.
The river or the bridge?

Sleep, easy and dangerous both
At every turn:

Which tonight?
A walk on the bridge, a swim

In the sharp teeth of the hungry water—
The choice is not mine.

I lie down to sleep and wait,
But sleep itself seems unwilling

To let me enter. Sleep itself
Taking care of me

The way they say that sleep does, sleep
The best medicine, the best doctor,

This singular curative
Dispensed by the centuries.

2

But, sleep will not let me enter.
In spite of its best efforts, behind it,

Somewhere, I hear the roar of the water in one ear,
And the bridge of dreams, the other thing,

I feel it under the soles of my feet.
I am called to both of them, led to them,

In spite of sleep
Not letting me move toward sleep. I hear the zoo

Animals behind the wall
Sleep stands in front of.

I am pushed and pulled, led by the clear, loud sound
In one ear,

And the soft, polished, slippery, moving wood of the bridge
Under one foot.

Soon enough, I enter, eager for embrace
Despite all else.

As I am able,
I stand on the invisible floor of the night.

WOMB-RIDER

1

He had been a guest, polite enough
All those many months,
A guest in the guise of a child.

But he was a man straightaway,
And came out already packed,
Packed and ready to move on.

He had been a hobo on a train,
Though how he had found this space
Remained a mystery.

If there was a child,
Nobody knew what had happened to it,
Only that this man was not the one.

But if he was not a child, then what a man he was.
He left town before anyone could ask
Any questions. He simply tipped his hat,

Counted his money, tied his shoes,
Then off he went, faster than anyone
Could follow. He was thought to have said

Goodbye, but accounts differ.
The mother, certainly, was inconsolable
Though the man had been quite handsome.

I knew something was happening, something
Strange, she said in confidence afterward.
I did not sing to the baby—it sang to me.

And how it knew the words, I did not understand.
Remembering those songs now
I feel better, it's true. They were so beautiful.

I think he was preparing me.
Where I should have been gathering clothes,
Fixing a room and a bed, thinking of a name,

I felt instead the need to do other things.
To eat more sophisticated foods,
To go to the movies and read about the theater.

I could feel him pushing me out the door
Some nights, as if he were bored.
I felt the urge more than once to drink,

Though I never had drunk before.
And it wasn't just his singing
That kept me awake, not just the music

I had never heard before
But which I found charming enough
And so let him continue.

No, it was the plans he made
Out loud, so loud I could hear them,
Hear him plotting out one adventure

And another, a life far from here—
Sometimes he spoke his plans in French,
French I think it was, to make the point of going away.

And he had money, too—that is,
He had suggested I set aside a certain amount
Each week, something for him,

And I did. Only the money turned out not to be
Money for diapers and oatmeal.
He knew just where to look for it on his way out.

Just like a man, I thought, just like a man—
I could see he was made for the world
Already. I had no tears

To say goodbye—he had taken those, too,
But he had extracted them
One night at a time.

Still, I cannot say they were tears of pain,
Tears of sorrow—quite the opposite.
They were tears of love, every one.

4

Reports differed in later years
Regarding what this man looked like—
Man or *child*, people used both terms.

Some say he simply left,
Not even bothering to tip his hat,
Nor did he turn to look backward even once as he went.

Others said just the opposite,
That he smiled, and that he lingered,
In fact, on the far side of the town.

To what purpose is again confused.
It was to get the drink he had waited for
So long, some said, and this made sense.

Others said that he met someone,
That all his words were new
And thereby made an impression,

Something favorable on all those who listened,
Attractive especially to the ladies who gathered around him.
Had he not spoken intimately to one woman

For hours and hours on end? Hours and weeks and months?
Had he not been inside a woman so much
He seemed like a dream?

5

He folded his parts out
Like so many umbrellas.
Some said it was more like a photographer's tripod—

Everyone had seen one of those. Tripod or umbrellas,
Whichever it was, everyone at least agreed:
He had been neatly packed.

Where he went afterward nobody could say.
The woman who had carried him
Had another child soon thereafter,

Since she had the room ready,
Both in the house and inside herself.
It was a room that needed to be filled,

Everyone agreed. Otherwise
This man would have ruined her,
The way she loved him.

There are other worlds, she said later,
There are other things going on.
Other lives happening at the same time,

Lives tangled up inside out with ours,
I'm certain of it.
Some of us get mixed up with each other.

6

In the small towns of the northern desert,
The towns that must make their own
Science and medicine and rumor,

Something mixed-up was the best explanation
For a man who comes and goes
The way this curious one did.

Sometimes a fraction of a dream
Solves something in the daytime.
On occasion, an arm reaches out

From some other place to scare us,
To scare us or to help steady us
When nothing else will, all those things out there:

Angels and werewolves, ghosts, lost
Souls, womb-riders and child-snatchers,
Bloodsuckers and all manner of distraught beings.

The man after all these years
Is almost forgotten, he left so fast,
And in the middle of so many other men.

People tell many stories of strange men
Coming into town. But the story of one
Leaving, this is still a little bit of news.

TWO

Wherever we sit these days is a
waiting room.

FEEDING THE COMPOST HEAP

Dried teas and sweet peels, shriveling rinds and still-wet fruit—
The compost gatherings speak something to the day and whimper

In the night, alive with their odd congress, this meeting of sours,
Blackness, citrus yellows, coffee grounds, hard sticks and green

Leaves half-brown, onion skins and onion itself, apple and orange
Seeds, pear stems and cut grass, old pomegranates and carrot.

What I eat, that heap has eaten. What I like, it gets, but less of.
It drinks rooibos and Ceylonese teas, French roast coffee—it drinks,

It tastes them, too. But in this way, it does not understand me.
What I don't like, it receives much of, and must think the worst of me.

It chokes where I choked, but I did not finish the meal it faces now,
The meal its dinner and breakfast, its lunch for weeks, for months.

It thinks me curious in my likes, and does not understand my dislikes,
Which are its world, those bits the makers of its great, beating, old

Prunish heart, half skin, half rot, something alive, purpling at its core,
Making something, keeping something, struggling, slow with slow.

A white rabbit of vapors emerges every now and then out of the bin,
A chuff of suddenness, a quick wheeze, a long-leap sigh that lingers.

I have watched this heap as if it were a child growing. From stiff hay,
Sprouting thick and unbendable, to spiderweb moved by my breath,

Nuanced by the slightest breeze, my walking by, by my hand,
That slight shiver every time. From stiff hay to moving web,

Bristle to wisp, bone to chalk: I have watched it grow smaller, away
From the shapes of things, into something else—an opposite child.

It lays a warm hand on the cool brow of me, heating things up,
Making a mulch, a loam, a darkness that says, *We'll start again.*

THE LEUKEMIA GIRLS

1

Sisters, daughters of the youngest
Daughter of my neighbor—it's confusing,

The girl at the end of the street in the old neighborhood,
My neighbor who was a friend, a friend of many years,

And whose mother was a friend of my father's
Since high school—it is exhausting to explain people,

Having to work so hard to invent them for someone else.
We do it anyway, and take a great deal of time trying.

These people, the people whose stories we tell
Each other, they're all like places on a map, the real directions

Told to us by someone else, by hard work and concentration,
That person pointing a finger and nodding a head at critical turns

You must be sure to make by particular trees—don't miss that turn—
The directions exhausting, finally, both to give and to get.

So it will do only to say that my friend's daughter
And her other daughter as well, both got leukemia.

2

Nobody knows why. There are answers, of course,
But the answers aren't answers. They are not answers

The way we think answers should be—yes ma'am,
No sir, well behaved and nice to be around.

41

Science may be our best way of understanding the world,
But it may not be our best way of living in it.

The answer is, nobody knows.
All that's left is to tell this story, to point at it,

Two girls, two daughters, two sisters:
To tell this story and to take the trouble it requires

To invent these two girls—again, and again, for the world—
And to say as directions, *I wouldn't go there,*

Stranger, not if I could help it.
But what to do? Even that caution is exhausting,

Knowing what I know about that house,
Knowing what I know about what I don't know.

SOMETIMES IT RAINS

The ready perfumes of summer's middle days,
Creosote, creosote after rain, rain

Bringing up the last of the orange-blossom smell,
The droplets of water rousing the fallen leaves

Enough to make a moment come back to life in them,
A second once more of something, a moment from when

They were white and waxy and alive with themselves.
But night comes, too, to gather this moment,

Even as we want it to stay, even as we will not go inside.
The creosote, the orange blossoms, the hot honeysuckle

Flowers in the desert moonlight, the shadows of yucca,
Those sharp fronds, they make a full burst of daggers

Black on the gray-colored ground of the early evening.
The ocher and pink colors of this place in daytime

Are parts of one color at night, so that to see them
One has to breathe in. And breathing in:

This has the curious effect of rain itself in that moment—
The smell rousing us to what we know inside ourselves.

But that is not the end of it, a rainy day turning itself
Into a moist evening full of crickets.

This place is no different from any other, and rain is rain
Here as much as anywhere. But something happens

In the desert after rain has come. We sleep a good sleep
That night. In the morning, we get up and find ourselves

Standing on the shore of the new world. In the desert,
We watch, if we're careful, and when we point at everything

We are complicit in the great magician's trick of the rain:
Rain falls down wet and gets up green.

EL ESPLENDOR

I was a boy. It was a Saturday.
At the top of a fine hill's rise in the high desert,

In the yellow-blossoming creosote and gray-green brush,
There was a picnic, a civic event intended to be festive,

The kind the Fifties invented, something right, the right thing to do,
Something new, something to feel something again After the War.

Here, it was people taking themselves out of regular downtown buildings
To make fires in pits, for *barbacoa*, the gift of a pig roasted for days,

And which people talked about for weeks,
And which I have remembered for years.

My parents took me and my brother to this hotel for movie stars
To eat the dripping *barbacoa* and hot tortillas on the outskirts of Nogales.

The hotel was in the rolling, horse-country north hills,
Not close enough to be walking distance,

So the thrill was that one had to arrive at this hotel by car—or horse,
or in a car that made somebody feel like they were on a horse, all

Muscle and sweat, whoever it was stepping out stringy haired and uncertain,
Feeling something between all right and pretty good.

This town was still in between in all things, with cars that ran on four legs,
Cars that didn't care so much about glass in their windows.

The hotel was called El Esplendor, though later because of a movie
They called it the Rancho Grande. In those names,

It was a place and a feeling both. Movie stars liked the entryway,
The blue-and-black-tiled fountain edged with a rim of trailing green rot.

Movie stars liked it and so did I, this cooling great room, this sea bottom
On top of the desert. The sound of the fountain changed this place.

This particular morning, we walked outside, all of us,
To the edge of the hill this place sat on,

To the great edge of the whole of the wandering Santa Cruz Valley,
A view that would find its way into movies, the imagination

Struck by the imagination.
John Wayne was there. Maybe not today, but often enough.

The day was warm. There were movie stars everywhere.
I stood with one foot up on a rock. My hands were on my hips.

My new jeans fit as if they were made for me, made for me
Right at that moment, not too long, too short, too tight, or too big.

As I surveyed the valley, took its measure with my ten-year-old eye,
Breathed its space into me, into my lungs and arms and heart,

I felt as great as I ever had, as perfect and hungry as I ever would.
It was a Saturday, and every Saturday since.

THAT STRANGE MAN, NIAL

Twice a week and sometimes more
He came to visit my mother after my father died.
He worked with machines and made a grease path
Through the house
Slightly but everywhere,
The chairs getting dark where he sat.

He had started his visits as a help to my mother
When my father was still alive,
My father having lost his sight,
Having lost his humor,
Having lost so much of who he had been
That who he had been was another man.

That strange man Nial promised at the funeral
He would not let my mother be alone.
What kind of declaration that was
We could only guess, simple as it sounded
And simple in the way he kept it
Even when we wanted him not to.

THE BIRDS THAT FLY FROM
THIS MOUTH

1

It is always right now—not a while ago, and not
In just a while. It is never yesterday.

Tomorrow is a country I have not visited,
And may not. Packing for that journey,

I think only of problems. Now, always now:
They tell me this is the sickness I inhabit.

I am stuck inside the house of myself, my address,
My small garden, squarely in that place between

What I remember and what I can guess.
It used to be that I could recall what used to be,

And I've always been able to imagine
What's going to be, what will happen tomorrow

In order to make plans.
But those feelings, their directions, they've gone.

They feel cleanly precised away from me,
Falling through a drain inside, running

Down my legs into the ground
Before I could catch hold of them.

It's always right now but I suspect there's more—
Something keeps wanting to come out of me,

But all I have is nothing in place of walking,
Looking instead of eating.

There aren't any other words that work.
I feel something, even if I can't say. I feel

What happened, what's going to happen, I think
I do, but no words come to me,

Even if I ask them to ask about lunch,
About dinner. I ask only small things of them,

These words. But they won't do it.
They tell a different story. It's somebody else talking.

Somebody always in a hurry. The words,
I hear them go and have their life: birds,

Every one, scattered suddenly into flight,
Making that small noise of theirs.

GOOD BONES LENT AND AT THEIR WORK STILL

1

His ribs—they are her hands
Remembered, her bones his bones now,

A moment of her from when she held him,
When he was small, when she held him

Just enough in her hands
He was held and not hurt—that forgotten,

Easy gift, her fingers
Still at their insistent work.

2

These ribs in him are the bones in his mother's fingers
Learned by heart. Her bones when she held him

Still hold him. Her fingers have grown larger in him,
More of her hands necessary to do the job of him now.

He remembers her there, in his bones,
Not by thinking but by feeling what they gave.

If he slouches, they hurt and make him sit up straighter.
If he runs too fast, they hurt and make him stop.

3

Whenever he desired it to be so, at his whimper
He could feel her fingers—those ten arms—come around him

In a grip, a grip menacing in all other circumstances,
The grip of an enemy's hands or a coyote's mouth,

Wild and long as fingers themselves—
But his whimper and her fingers were none of that.

This is what she left him, this feeling,
Her after she was gone.

4

His ribs, two ladders, two shutters, two
Trellises in the backyard garden.

Still, he has more than once closed the venetian blinds
Of them, felt the multiple, thin tines of their two rakes

Rasp him back
From harm,

Trying. If he leans over too quickly,
He has made a bellows of them.

5

If he sits up too quickly, now, an old man,
He makes of those bones an accordion, stretched,

A small sound, a breath taken in, a music.
That tiny noise, it is a comfort to her, even still.

It is in this way that they speak
Even after so many years:

Something sudden happens, something
Small, out of which a feeling comes.

THE OUTSIDE WOMAN

1

She was thick in the arms and with a stomach, strong enough
Working with the men, her brothers and her father quiet.

She got sweat marks on the swells, sweat
In the deep V of her chest, along the Y of her lower back,

The U under her arms and at the zipper of her jeans,
Spelling herself right like anybody.

When she walked in at the beginning of March
The doctor said, *You're pregnant,*

Like that, and *You'll have a baby
By the end of the month*, which she did,

A baby she called Ángel because what else.
But how could this happen? She started to say it

But everything moved so fast.
By the time the words came out

The baby had beaten them.
Her mother had looked at her hips:

They're too thin, she said, *too close together,
You'll never have children.*

And she believed her. With that and with a shrug
Of her shoulders and her eyebrows,

And with only a word
About the muscular gush of her quick childbirth

Being like the times she had stepped on the overripe melons,
Or the fattened green bodies of the June bugs too heavy

To lift themselves after a good season of rain and eating,
There was nothing else to say.

2

Two women can't be in labor at the same time—
They won't *dar la luz*. You know.

They won't *give the light.* So one had to go outside.
I was an outside woman.

That's how things were. In the fields
You had to understand the rules.

There were some easy ones, like shouting
¡Ho-rú-ga! to the ant lions in the sand.

That was their name and what you said to call them out,
Cupping your hands over their mounds. *Ant lion!*

Come out! You called them out loud
And you called them out twice, *Ant lion! Hey, ant lion!*

So that everybody—you and the animals and the trees,
Everybody—would know what was what,

That they were there and so were you.
You made a little fuss so that everybody knew

How to start the day, and when, and what to plan for.
The ant lions and the *niños de la tierra*, pink and baby-like,

I say baby-like because they cried,
These and the regular tarantulas and scorpions—

All of it—everything in Arizona—
Everything had its corner and its season.

3

Some things in the fields you picked for work,
Some things you picked for yourself.

Everybody knew.
No one said.

Bellotas, they were in June, July, picked
Before the August rains.

People called them acorns, but they didn't look like acorns
In the pictures in books in school.

These acorns made a different noise
And probably didn't fit in a picture.

These were maybe acorns from the regular oak here,
The scrub oak, not the mighty oak,

Whatever the mighty oak was. It was something
Somebody heard said once.

There were other nuts, little black nuts,
Black walnuts from the *nogal* trees.

And to chew while you worked, *pechitas*—
Mesquite beans, to chew, or to make *atole.*

Then there were the things you picked because you had to.
Pecans in November and December,

Before the winter rains. Pecans
In Continental, grapes in Tubac.

Picking cotton, lettuce, cantaloupes, peanuts
By Green Valley, onions, which stank, and cotton

And lettuce in Marana. Cantaloupes in Eloy,
Elotes in Willcox, peaches in Elfrida.

It wasn't so much with me, but my brother was picking
Since eight years old. I had a little longer.

4

There was school. What I did on my summer vacation:
Kids said things like that they learned how to swim.

Kids said a lot of things, but I didn't.
I could have, but I didn't.

¡Ho-rú-ga! I knew right away was no good here,
So I never said it. I never said

Any of the things I knew, and that was a lot
Not to say. It was the measure of my quiet.

THE OLD WATER HUSBAND

Water is always hungry and we are always thirsty.
We and water together have come through the centuries

To make certain exchanges with each other—our bodies,
For example: We have given them over to one another, taking,

Giving, in a rhythm of centuries, kelp and eyes, shells and hands,
The line between us measured by the tender widths of our skins,

The paper of our small contract of need. Water, that great animal,
Us, that great animal—together we have made a long marriage,

Like it or not, a little unsure of each other, tired sometimes,
Unsteady, perhaps, but still, every day wanting more than there is.

NIGHT COMES TO THE DESERT

Like the sun growing dim on the far stone rim of the hill
In the slight-chill stillness of the darkening earth,

The coming quiet thrill of coolness sung is the last song
Sound of the birds, and surprising. The house finches,

Grackles, the fast hummingbirds and slow pigeons,
All of them who had been in flight all day, a full day,

They finish the work of making the night into a nest
Fixed and filled enough for what comes next,

Their song, words long in the mouth of them,
Ready enough for their life in the dark, their life

In the half-hard hours that lie ahead, their nesting bed
Slept-in with eyes open, led more by noise than light.

Theirs is a sleep so like ours in the city, the sleep of us,
So many who are in their way these birds and this day.

THE OLD WAIT

As we find ourselves together for the old wait,
Hold my hand while you can—

Sit down, *so simple,* with me.
We are bereft of much, but not all:

We have what is left, what is us.
We understand we are not the first.

Here we are again in a waiting room—
This time it is our house.

You and I,
Wherever we sit these days is a waiting room.

Those who leave us leave
By sitting down as we sit down.

We must remember to get up, not to get
So comfortable with ourselves.

We don't want to stand and start the walk
Toward what comes next,

To take our turn. But we must.
We must for now. It is for us to do.

THOSE BEFORE ME

When one of us goes,
Sweet, I feel weaker

As together I had felt strong,
Fuller with the more of me

You made, two adding up to
More than one, and three—

Who could stop us? But,
Take us away from each other,

Then the game is new.
The instruction manual—now

There's nobody to ask—
The instruction manual, again,

Is nowhere to be found.
Onward, I say, in spite of this,

Loudly, *onward,* steadfast,
But I do not mean it

The way I have meant things,
The way things should be meant.

THREE

We spend our lives imagining other-
wise.

MY DOG, THAT STRANGER

1

Fallen, low, pooled, and lurking smells gather at a dog's eye-level,
Things his eyes do not see but which his nose guarantees him are there,

Enough to stop him, scents and molds and rots that make him lurch, pink
Blotches of floor-sugar calling *Hey you* to him, loud enough for his ears

To hear through his nose. His eyes, old things, he knows they mean well,
And they try, but his nose is how he sees the world, and tastes, and hears it.

2

Some loud smells scare him at first, but they call him back, they call
His name—*How did they know it?* They reach out to him, those sirens

He cannot resist, even against all impulse toward home. *Hey, boy,* coolly
They say, and he goes, no matter where. And when he goes, he goes

Fast. And when he gets to them, his nose is the first on the scene. It's why
Dogs have long noses—they can't wait to get where they want to get.

3

But when they get there, they're there, and it's just a smell. All they can do,
Crazy dogs, is turn in circles. They look up at us, after a while, to whimper:

Where did it go, and why, and why did it not take me. The circling stops,
Finally, and the ears go up when we call, but the way back is slow.

As things turn out, urinating on everything in sight did not help. Bereft,
Eyes up, they come back into consciousness, shaking their heads.

The ghosts of everything good do not give up, however. They lie in wait
Up the walk, a wet, prunish mark, an invisible, dried sweat, a potato chip.

The calm seas newly restored in the soul of the dog, they do not last,
Not even for a minute. *Hey,* he hears again through both his nostrils,

Those precision instruments wrinkling themselves to the left, then up
Slightly, unsure at first, then fixed. *Hey you,* says a new voice—*you.*

My dog does not belong to me. My dog is not mine every day
For a few minutes. For that time I belong to him, my teacher, that small

Wagging grace. I watch the simple and not simple. He smells something
From so many centuries past, all in the few seconds of a small moment,

That dark joy, smudges on leaves, the beetle shell with ants, old snake:
Hey you, they repeat. *Yeah, what?* he answers. I wait to hear his news.

THE NIGHT OF NO AIRPLANES

We walk out into the light dark of the evening,
My son and I, so many times before

Having walked here, so many years and reasons.
The steps are easy and not many.

We stand by the ash tree, which has not grown
In the ten years since we planted it.

The tree is sickly, I suppose, and still
It is what I have sometimes wished onto my son—

That he might have stayed
All the ways I have known him, that baby,

That boy, that young man shaving in the bathroom.
But the tree is a good reminder, having no more leaves

Than it ever had, no more of anything. Together,
Our job tonight is not the tree, but to look up,

To look for airplanes tonight,
Our own ancient practice, my son's and mine,

A night that has been reported in the news
As not having any.

UNCOVERED ANTS

Lifting a rotting landscaper's log full of craggy wood-spikes, a treasure
Shows—fresh red and the straw color of gold, they glitter then glimmer,

Ants everywhere, thick, unsunned, small and new to the greater world,
They move like a honey poured, so many kids on the last day of school

Bursting out the door: I was one of those boys from years ago. I knew
What being in the middle of something like this felt like—

There was no middle. Instead, a hundred edges, a hundred mouths,
Two hundred legs, single-minded but not with a single mind:

Each of us had a plan not bigger than getting the heck out of there.
It was a good plan, and we were committed to it, running, pushing

As if we had all this time been holding our breath hard underwater,
Swimmers up at the very last moment bearable, hard and sudden

In a reverse scream, drawing into us all the possible air and noise
The moment had to offer, drawing into us what fear could push out.

This was a category of happiness, the opposite of scared, a moment, joy.
Did these ants feel it, too? Right now, sudden, finally, like me that day

Throwing open the doors and running into the arms of the world?
They were ants, only ants, what I was looking at. But for a moment

I felt myself in them, the frenzied grammar of childhood, the feeling
Going out that door gave me. I did not see my face in them, but I saw

My arms. Still, they were ants, and soon enough crawling everywhere.
I returned the rotting log to its quietude, to its attitude of decorum—

A frame for the yard the way one might frame and hang a painting,
This log, full of life, one more part of the garden getting old.

THE HUNDRED-THOUSAND-THING DAY

It began so quietly.
It ended with sleep.

In between was not the thunder of a hundred thousand things in a row,
Not so much noise and static and kelp, spiderweb and broken glass—

Those things
That stop us.

This day was not
That day.

The hundred thousand things that happened to him, happened every one
In a carpenter's instant, a hand stopping when a thing is smoothed,

The moment so small
It was a fingersnap,

A moment
Made from bee-sting.

All those things, they felt like something, something all at once, *ouch*,
A back-lot pack of dogs, twenty minnows turning on a dime, sharp,

So many,
So fast,

So much.
A hundred

thousand things are what he felt when he saw her eyes, then heard them,
first look, casual to anyone else, but then her look a second time,

Her eyes' *yes,*
That single word.

THE RAIN THAT FALLS HERE

The rain that falls here is lost,
Having meant surely to fall somewhere else,

Somewhere that's already green.
Like always, like last season,

Like next season—someplace rich with green.
Water knows what to do

And wants a comfortable life
Like anyone.

This time, its instructions get mixed up.
The wind, just to do something different

And as a joke, indifferent and bored,
Carries it here. Pelicans get lost

This same way, blown off course from California.
They get caught standing on the highway medians

Not knowing what to do as the cars speed by.
Like rain, pelicans make the news that evening.

The green that the rain saw and meant to feed—
That easy job it thought to have,

Driving around in those big Cadillac clouds,
Not asking anyone for directions—looking down,

The green it thought it saw was something else here.
The green it saw was spray paint and mirage,

Old glass, tired plastic, turquoise and roadkill.
As it turns out, the green that lives here is hard,

Dried and full of dirt just as hard. Sometimes
A few green leaves show themselves,

But not easily. A few peach beetles fly around
Carrying green to taunt us,

A few horseflies are green colored. Dried-up
Cowponds have some green around the lip

Of their brown shore, and the man-made lakes
Keep some reeds up for decoration.

3

There are golf courses, to be sure, all green,
But nobody is fooled by them.

They don't count in this discussion.
Anything green here is underground, waiting

To come up, a small guerrilla army of grasses
And wildflowers, scrub brush and cactus.

And people. People would turn green and grow
If there were water, plenty of rain.

We're not sure about this, as it has never happened.
But there is something, just under the skin here,

Something more than sweat. There is a green
Inside, waiting to change everything.

People from other places would not know—
They have used up their allotment of green.

But those here, who have waited these centuries,
That layer of skin they can't explain, it's there.

THE SWEET SALT SEA

In the desert, water is not water
The way water finds itself
Next to itself
In the sea.

In the desert, water is always thirsty—
It cannot get enough of itself,
Cannot drink at the well
It has evaporated from.

In the desert, water runs but does not run
Quickly, and yet no one
Catches it quickly, not quickly
Enough, not easily, not enough, never enough.

In the desert, water is not the hunter
But hunter of its place, hunting down,
And we hunt down
For it and follow it and find it and swallow it.

In the desert, water gets hotter
Than it should, hotter than it can, hot
So that we are not always sure of its name, or its touch,
The dream of water never the same as what we've got.

In the desert, water, when there is water, water is the concert:
It makes happen the grass skirt and sport shirt,
Flirting of the coyote and the brown wren, the lizard
That crawls on the hardpan dirt and the hawk come down from the sky.

In the desert, heat makes the asphalt shimmer, heat dreaming
Water even at its work. The pelicans that have lost their way
Find this dream, and mistake it for what it seems to be: In joy, they dive
Into the highway, looking for the black fish of cruelty.

In the desert, water tolerates us all, lets us do what we will
With it. It makes a sweet salt sea, half dry and half wet, half
Dream and thirst, half early August lightning and rain, half water, half
Nothing, one eye out of two when looking at the things of this place.

THE FULL AUGUST AFTERNOON
MORNING

It was a simple summer thunderstorm, but in its simplicity it covered
     the sky
End to end, side to side, making a circus of those underneath looking
     up at the tent.

Morning mattered no more than afternoon—the darkness was
     its own time,
Defined not by minute hands or slow hours but by hammers of rain
     and noise and light:

This was, and suddenly, the world of now. What came before and what
     would come
Afterward, none of it mattered, none of it was bigger than this
     attention we paid.

This simple demand of the world, it constituted no tragedy—it was
     only a thunderstorm,
After all, requiring after so many centuries of experience no wringing
     of the hands.

But it made an appointment to be respected, and left nowhere else to
     go, everything
In its stoppage—no electricity, no traction, no dry clothes, no quiet
     place, no fire.

As if the lake had risen all at once into it, the sky seemed a great,
     moving gray water,
The floor and the ceiling of this small world moved in sudden
     exchange, reversed—

Had we fallen over upside down?—We hadn't. It was the lake after all
       up there, risen,
Actual, out of bed into the sky hanging, floating, suspended as if it
       belonged and could,

The great wafting waves now clouds easily enough, our eye a boat on
       that vastness.
The waves–the clouds–the waves, they were waves, the menacing kind,
       whose hands

Shake you—they shake you, they prod, they drive, those rough,
       impatient boys' hands
Playing a piano by pushing it, pounding, hitting its parts to make an
       unbreakable music,

The music that thunder is, that loud-so-much, so many hard sounds that
       one feels them,
The fist of the sky at our face, hitting our raised and wincing ears so that
       they squint

Every time as if they were eyes closing at a sharp light, ears hurt, ears
       unwilling,
Closed by the square whisper of the piano music turned inside out into
       shout,

Making the thing said, said loudly, but not heard, the song sung, but too
       much of it, not
Understood, too much sound and light, too much world in a moment
       like this.

PERFECT FOR ANY OCCASION

1

Pies have a reputation.
And it's immediate—no talk of potential

Regarding a pie. It's good
Or it isn't, but mostly it is—sweet, very sweet

Right then, right there, blue and red.
It can't go to junior college,

Work hard for the grades,
Work two jobs on the side.

It can't slowly build a reputation
And a growing client base.

A pie gets one chance
And knows it, wearing as makeup

Those sparkling granules of sugar,
As a collar those diamond cutouts

Bespeaking Fair Day, felicity, contentment.
I tell you everything is great, says a pie,

Great, and fun, and fine.
And you smell nice, too, someone says.

A full pound of round sound, all *ahh,* all good.
Pies live a life of applause.

2

But then there are the other pies.
The leftover pies. The ones

Nobody chooses at Thanksgiving.
Mincemeat? What the hell is that? people ask,

Pointing instead at a double helping of Mr.
"I-can-do-no-wrong" pecan pie.

But the unchosen pies have a long history, too.
They have plenty of good stories, places they've been—

They were once fun, too—
But nobody wants to listen to them anymore.

Oh sure, everybody used to love lard,
But things have changed, brother—things have changed.

That's never the end of the story, of course.
Some pies make a break for it—

Live underground for a while,
Doing what they can, talking fast,

Trying to be sweet pizzas, if they're lucky.
But no good comes of it. Nobody is fooled.

A pie is a pie for one great day. Last week,
It was Jell-O. Tomorrow, it'll be cake.

ELSEWHERE, SOMETIMES

1

Orion appears always-bright in my sky
No matter what, that vivid

Small line regular in my irregular nights
No matter, it seems to me, the season,

No matter the clouds. The three stars
In the belt, they are always first seen,

The first recognized, the first familiars of the sky,
The initial shore of a vast black.

The Big Dipper is next, north if you know how
To find it, trustworthy, but taking a second

Or two more to fix on. I'm glad it's there.
It's more help to me than Orion. But still,

I do not go to it first. That's how we are,
All of us. I thought it was just me, but it's all of us.

2

Orion was Samuel Clemens's brother's name.
The Big Dipper is called *La Casserole* in French.

What is ours and what is profound to us,
These moments are meaningless

To someone else, or else different. Everything
Said differently, with different words,

Other people up in the sky, different
Ways to think about the world.

Some things are science, and good to know:
The volume of Earth's moon is the same

As the volume of the Pacific Ocean.
Some things simply are what they are:

Buzz Aldrin, the second man on the moon in 1969—
His mother's maiden name was Moon.

3

Orion appears always-bright in my sky,
Those three stars, that ellipsis

Suddenly clear—the stars it has omitted,
The stars it has implied,

I have found them: in lake water,
Their reflection, so many of them,

They make confetti in the water.
We have looked up for stars, finally,

Without thinking. We have not looked
Sideways, not down, not at each other.

But here is another science: I blink,
Blink three times. I see stars in that moment,

Unnamed and many, these constellations
From the dark of closed eyes, the dark of sleep.

4

The stars are other places as well, every direction,
Everywhere. They are all the eyes

In the world, every beast, all those eyes
Opening and closing and opening.

They are the static I have heard
In between stations on a radio.

When my hand goes to sleep, when I move it,
When that hand seems suddenly desperate

To come alive,
It is stars that burst in my hand.

In that moment, I am made of them,
Loud, more than water, more than bones.

What I feel in my hand is what I see in the sky,
Is how I touch and by which I feel that sky.

LUNAR ECLIPSE: ARIZONA, 2004

We expected red, some old-sky orange, some noise—
We got something else instead, some other world's eclipse,

Something from some other newscast, someone else's newspaper.
Ours was a watercolorist's story of an eclipse,

Early evening black-and-white and the other color
That connects opposites, but which is not a particular color

Itself, just that gray again in so many shades. Television used to
Look this way, and photographs, and smoke from trains.

The moon through the clouds had the slightly ruffled edging,
Its white a wan color, suffering water saturation, looking

The way watery colors extend outward on and all over a canvas,
Like the edges of a small cabbage leaf everywhere.

Cabbage, but no green, or green so muted and so far away
It was just one more shade of gray, and faded, even then.

All of us watched the moon's eclipse tonight
And wondered that in this new century it did not entertain us.

A LIGHTNING FIRE OUT OF SEASON

The smoke, a late winter fire, rises in a line on the western horizon.
The smoke looks like the steam from an old movie train engine,
The illusion of industry, the impression of sturdy movement.

But this fire, it is not ours, as so much of the world as well
Is not. The smudged, long line of smoke in the distance:
It is nature's train, the season's engine, heat's need—

Not ours. We spend our lives imagining otherwise.
But the world: The world will do what it chooses.
In this shadow, we are left to do what we can.

SEVEN HARD SEASONS

Easy enough at first, the new season tracks fallen leaves into the house.
It comes in cold, with a coat and a shiver,
Sometimes wet.
The season before this one leaves not bold but with a tremor
Roused in the knees, falling as slow as it can toward winter's
Hardest bite.
The things of the world fold inward, then, grieving in whimpers, simmers
On a stovetop, hunched inside themselves for warmth, on the outside old,
Bright light bright
Only in the painting on the curl of the alcove wall.
Otherwise, summer and spring fail. They do not
Come tonight
Out of turn, not yet, still in the distance, unwilling, away and off.
Winter is itself seven hard seasons, or eight, a stopped time uncharted,
Dirty white,
Gray then brown, night in snow, spare limbs and hard
Steps, winter different from other seasons, its measures sure,
Silhouette
Shadows through dim days pushing us to sit, perhaps to walk no farther,
Winter not part of but more than a year, and without ease, or end,
Or regret.
But that darkness: do not give over to it, or count as one more drowned.
And so this, only this, however small: Socks up and jacket tight, my love,
Jacket tight.

FOUR

I will do what I can.

BEETLES AND FROGS

The peach beetles bring green
With them. They wear it and nothing else

On their backs, green
Trimmed with fine yellow stripes.

Frogs, too, bring green with them,
Frogs and hummingbirds under the wing.

In the green they harbor and look after: green,
Black and dark blue, red and yellow,

With these colors each animal carries with it
News from one world to another.

We think they are bringing the news to us.
Save for our loyal dogs, however,

And sometimes a cat, animals do not
Stop in front of us. They run

Instead. They fly and hop, crawl and yip.
Everything they do, they do away from us.

To whom do they deliver this news, then?
And how much news has there been?

And what is the hurry, the incessant effort,
Everything moving so continually around us?

The sun at its work every day does not stop
For us. The moon does not stop.

The birds are in a hurry all the time,
In a rush to reach their perch on a branch

In the congress they hold at all hours
In the linden trees, and the tamarisks,

All those birds speaking simultaneously,
Without translation for us, any of us,

Not one single word directed toward us,
No bird asking us for anything.

Worms carrying dirt, ants in their trails,
Fish schooling in perfect formation

For something, this practice we mimic
So ungracefully with our soldiers,

Moving left, moving right, walking all
Together, but for what?

Everything moves and will not stop.
It exhausts us. We take vacations.

We sit in Adirondack chairs,
Shaking our heads as we watch the world—

Silly thing! And all those animals.
We shake our heads and cluck our tongues

At this mysterious, incessant business
The world seems so insistent upon.

DARK-HAIRED MEN

My father was a dark-haired man,
Lucky for him,

Lucky in the eyes of my mother,
Her parents, and the whole town

In the whole of England
Where my Mexican father was stationed

At the end of one war
And the beginning of another.

He was a paratrooping medic,
My mother a nurse.

They dated, they dated
Two years, days and nights.

New Year's Eves in England
My father was a wanted man,

The luck of a dark-haired man, they said,
That's what you'd get

If you got one to cross over your threshold
Before midnight.

They were right, everybody who thought that.
They were right.

The cold of those nights
Shivered out the ghosts,

Steam coming out of people's mouths.
But what are ghosts if not that:

They are what's inside us,
After all. They are what we keep warm.

We breathe them out, but only a little,
Knowing one day it will be us.

The luck of a dark-haired man,
I believe it.

ARIZONA, THE SUN, AND WHAT
THAT'S LIKE

1

April in Arizona, the orange blossoms
In heat, their scent makes bees of us all.

The corners of the great American southwest,
The orange and brown bricks, the lazy half-blue

Jacaranda, the red bougainvillea everywhere,
Thorny behemoths of the Great Mexican North,

That blood color, so much on so many white walls,
The smells of creosote, the coyote sounds at night—

This place, everything, gives itself freely to you.
Everything sings its own song, strange and plain.

But a cloudy day—don't believe it:
There are no cloudy days.

2

When the sky looks cloudy, when it's one of those days,
It's the sun, the sun up to no good and behind everything,

Itching for a little fun at your expense.
If it looks like rain, don't say so out loud. Everyone will laugh.

The sun is just trying to pass itself off, to get close to you
By wearing stick-on mustaches and false beards,

Trying to make itself up to look like clouds, the mustache
Wisps, the gray beard, and the hairy paunch—

The sun will try everything in the book,
But it's never very good at it, everything so theatrical

With rental thunder-and-lightning machines
Pounding off in the distance. It's always overdone.

3

That's how the sun does things, over the top.
When there are clouds, or those things that look like clouds,

The sky is like someplace else's sky, not ours,
Someplace that knows the subtleties of shifting weather.

It's true there are so many clouds, especially
Late summer, so many clouds that it looks like a wet sky,

Rain imminent, happy like the impending arrival of a favorite
Uncle with ice cream. But don't be fooled—nobody else here is.

Those aren't clouds. There are no clouds. They are the cheap
Hand puppets of a lazy sun, a spoiled only child

Who doesn't want to get up and get dressed yet,
Tossing its toys, its stuffed animals, up into the air for fun.

4

The winter that comes is weak, too tired like us
From the heat, so that it, as well, sits in a corner

Looking for shade, one more dog dreaming of a river.
If the clouds are not clouds here, neither is the sun

The sun here. That spot in the sky is a magnifying glass
Through which the sun is focused behind it.

And we, we are all ants here, in this version of things.
We try to hide, to condition the air,

To move about in cars, or else slowly and with water bottles.
We build patios onto the city.

But sooner or later we feel it, the inhuman, unrelenting,
Circus-strongman strength on the flimsy barbell that is us.

5

But like ants, we learn to lift the heat ourselves, the heat,
Which is twenty times our size. We crawl on all our legs,

We watch our arms and eyebrows become feelers,
All of us, in the two seconds of darkness,

That half-second dream that we have
In the moment we step outside

And the sun makes us close our eyes.
Inside, we watch television.

It's always the weather
And traffic reports, the lines of cars

All ants, in those trails we laugh at
When we think it isn't us.

6

Rivers here are mean, and taunt us.
They promise something they don't deliver.

Rivers are the desert's workhorses, its beasts.
A river is the desert's mule.

And the sun, the sun is that mule's life.
Walking in the sun makes you feel

You're carrying a weight, a whole
Other person who is carrying

Another whole person on your back,
As if you were a stack of Harris hawks,

The way they stand on each other's shoulders.
All this weight, like the water in the rivers, invisible.

7

The Harris hawks sit on each other's shoulders
To show you how, to prepare you.

They've lived in the desert a long time.
If the sun makes you feel things,

It makes you see things, too. A tree in the distance,
A green something, some water—

None of this is true. It's all a trick of this place.
The sun makes you see these things,

Holds them out like a carrot
In front of the donkey: you, the mule,

The beast, to make you keep walking.
And you do. Nobody knows why.

THE BOLEROS

My love—they always begin the same way,
These songs in Spanish—*My love, it hurts.*

Mi amor, you've gone away and it hurts.
That you stay, hurts. It hurts

That I'm going away. It hurts that I have to stay.
It hurts no matter which way we move—

It hurts, but none of that matters,
Because of what comes next: *¡Ay! ¡Ay!*

The several words, the several sentences,
Never too many and not much, just enough

To turn the moment: They say,
Your love is like a sweet, homemade honey—

Usually—almost always—the words are better,
Much better, than *a sweet, homemade honey,*

And that's the thing—they work, like a wood screw
Into a two-by-four, each repetition another whole turn

Full of feeling, forced into you.
The words, and a half-sob as well

In the voice of the singer, they speak to you—
They somehow know your story

Even though you are strangers. These words,
You know them. They may be your secret.

That line, whatever it is, it doesn't work by itself—
It needs you. It points to, but does not say,

The smaller words, the rest of the story, all
The things that make us understand how it hurts,

Whatever it is. And saying it twice—that's all right.
We understand. We understand.

The why we got this way, and why it all hurts,
How life with you was all so good, whoever you are,

So that leaving you behind is a hard thing—
It's easy to listen to in a song.

Mi amor, mi amor. It's easy to feel
Sympathy for the singer, for Pedro Vargas,

For poor Lola Beltrán. We sing along and loud,
We listen to the words, say them again ourselves,

Happy, laughing. It's easy and makes us feel good
To let it be someone else's song.

FIRES IN THE NEWS

The fires aren't in the news anymore this summer. They were
Everything for weeks. They made good pictures and sad people.

The newspapers worked as tissue, the television as a loud town crier.
But the reporters have moved on, just like that, though the fires aren't out.

They're still burning. They've never been out, and will never go out.
Reporting fire on the news, it's a trick on us. The news about fire,

It is always old news. But the trick is on them, as well. The news on fire,
It will be the headline story in the paper again next summer, bright,

Shiny, a new television story with maps and interviews and solemn advice.
Though we remember this story from last time, still, we are kind.

We will all play along and try not to embarrass the newscaster,
A young man who is not from here, but who is serious and tries hard.

THINKING SOUP

I wanted to cook something, *she said to me,*
Taking out the neatly wrapped spices and the vegetables

To make some cocido *soup, one thing touched at a time,*
Some big ears of corn snapped in two, some yellow squash,

Some saved meat broth, some cabbage, some cut potatoes.
That's what's wrong with this neighborhood, *she said,*

Even the whole city—this place has lost its recipes.
Oh, you can find food, and people pretending to make it,

Pretending to mix things together by hand, pretending
That mix of vague, off-white powders makes the food you eat.

And you can't go and ask them at that place—you can't—
It's not as if they were your mother or your grandmother. No.

They won't tell you how to make what they put into packages.
They won't let you stand there and practice with them.

It's like that. Really, I don't think they know how.
I don't even think they know where the things they use—

The flour or the chicken—where any of it comes from,
Those people who work there. Those children.

That's part of it, too—they're all so young. I've heard that
The people you see don't even make these foods they sell.

The foods come from somewhere else, and what's in those packages,
It's a big mystery. As if chickens are a big mystery.

It's not a mystery. You just take a chicken by the throat,
Hold it firmly, and swing it around your head hard.

It's not a mystery except that maybe you turn your head away
So that even you don't look at what you're doing,

Knowing what you know you would see. Cooking soup,
That good soup of mine that you like, it's not as easy as it looks.

WHEN SHOPPING WAS EVERY DAY:
NOGALES, 1956

1

The fresh bananas in the *mercado,* the ones
Stacked next to the still-dirty onions and carrots

On one side, sugarcane and ripening figs on the other:
The fresh bananas here came in many shades,

Some yellow, some ocher and bluish, some red, deep
Red and as much purple as well, with some black.

We were used to seeing the yellows, but these others
Together could not sit still in that quiet frenzy of blush,

And shape, too, larger and smaller, Brazil-nut shaped,
Some of them, hard-looking and fatter than yellows.

They seemed to move in the bins from the noise they made.
They sold themselves, calling out to people,

Some of them large enough to reach out, as well,
As if they were bright parrots with curious beaks.

When someone jostled a bin and some of the bananas moved,
Hold on to your wallet was the best advice,

Those bananas in their loudness smart enough
In their quietude to have made an alternate plan for survival.

The *mercado* was like this in those days, the smells
Full of the taste of another world in those deafening colors,

A taste from high up in the branches,
And from the insides of the earth as well,

The insides and the far reaches of the thick roots
Laid out to taste here, to give us news. Red—

It told us those bananas came from somewhere else.
Still, to eat one, there had to be a frown, very big—

That child's way of first tasting anything.
Are you sure I should eat this? the frown says,

Because I don't think so. It doesn't seem
Quite right. It's not yellow, not like the others—

Are you sure you're a good mother? What if
Something happens to me? But mothers frown, too.

The red bananas were sweet to taste, ripe, and right,
And strange and deformed, and bruised and hard,

And small—all of this next to the yellow ones, all
This, while the yellow ones had only their yellow.

WITH FAMILY

I have had a family and been part of a family.
I have had a child and been a child.

I have loved my mother and my father,
My son and my daughter, my wife and my husband.

I'm not the only one.
There are others complicit in this scheme.

We have moved inexplicably through the years
Toward and away from each other—perhaps it was the moon.

But here we are now, a roomful of strangers,
We say. We introduce each other to each other.

What happens next happens every time.
We talk and then we are caught by some shiny thing

Like fish—but for us the hook is a curious name, a phrase,
The smells of coffee and orange blossoms,

The names of all the animals we have had,
Something about where you were born and where I was born.

This next part surprises us every time—
I am in your family tree and you are in mine.

If we can't find the connection going back a hundred years,
We will find it going back a thousand.

Through all those years I have gone by many names,
Tried on different clothes, painted myself different colors.

How lucky to have found each other again today,
How lucky, and how many stories we bring to tell,

So many of them happy, though some are not and will be news.
Hello, I say to you, again after all these centuries.

THE SONORAN HEAT, IN SUMMER
AND AT NIGHT

1

We should not wear clothes, but we do.
We have handkerchiefs for the sweat,

Great shows of lemonade for the throat,
Umbrellas for our heads in the daytime.

All of these, they work, but only in drawings,
Only as ideas, only for others

Far away from what really happens here.
These devices, they are never enough, almost nothing,

Though we do not give them up quickly
As even the quarter inch of relief they give,

The half second, the quick blink, is, even so quickly,
Not something to scorn or to turn down in this place.

2

The heat by July has started its mood
Pushing its right-side, stronger shoulder against us,

Holding us to the ground
Cheek to stone, relentless unmannered merciless.

Stay away from it.
It's worse than the darkness but inhabits all the same places,

Out there, always out there,
Its edges in evidence

All around us, about to envelop us,
Put its arms around us any moment and all the time,

Our doing the small things we do
To keep it at bay, not well, just barely.

3

Heat in the darkness with no one to see it,
It's unkind and without particular education

And therefore without fear, without understanding.
Everything for the heat is the same, not one thing and not another.

It is drunk with itself
And there are so many of us to hunt

It doesn't know whom to start with,
And doesn't care.

So, being quiet is the only thing.
Stay out of its way. Find cool sheets. Wet them even more.

Don't make any noise
That will draw it to you in the shadows.

4

Don't move. Don't breathe.
The heat, it doesn't matter when, it's always out there.

There is no worthy or effective complaint,
No salve against it.

When the heat comes to knock, some lumbering cousin
Having invited itself to visit for the hunting season,

This house is the far corner of everything once alive.
Nights in July-turned-to-August weigh the earth down.

We feel the sinking weight of this hot drunkenness,
The dizziness of the falling, all of us.

But we do not say so. We pretend
All is otherwise. It is the only way.

HAVING EATEN THAT WAY AGAIN

I am the commander of the suddenly portly vessel of myself,
Steering wide and slow and mostly forward, mostly

In a best effort to get through just the one next regular step, just
Enough to keep myself moving, hoping nobody will notice

The slow, or too fast, or lingering, approximate nature of my walk.
Tonight, I've just eaten too much. The balloon inside me, that thing

That feels like a balloon, or tire, has inflated, and I carry it carefully.
I shouldn't eat that much, but I do. And I do every time.

But the eating isn't what I'm thinking of—it's all the other
Approximations in front of me, all the lights blinking for attention

On this human steering control panel of me—*Get up,* they say, *shower,*
Shave, speak up, eat breakfast, pretend to know the person in the car

You wave to as you go out front with the dog to get the paper.
It is a drunkenness, eating so much. It is wine, stanching this hunger.

It is a weight, getting up at all. Getting up again and then again,
That is what I have eaten too much of. I am full by all of this,

Heavy with needing to do it every day. It's more than dinner,
It's always more than dinner, all of us, when we eat what we eat.

WALKING AND THINKING TOO NEAR

The thick and shrill of things, the busy days,
Even in them the small moment constantly happens:

The telling sound a shoe makes, for example,
Sudden, soft, sure on a gray and purple concrete,

The concrete itself soft and hard both, its surface cracked.
We avoid the cracks, and each crack dodged makes a rhythm

In the walking of the shoe, a half-belief made half-song
In the body of its wearer, in those legs,

In the mind engaged with the world at that moment
But remembering that the cracks in the sidewalk, too,

Might mean something after all, a mother's cracked back
Too real in recent experience, too close

To the things that happen in our lives, too near
The broken hip, the broken heart, the broken voice,

Too near, so that to step to the side of it all,
This is a prayer, this vigilant placing of the foot

That says with its step,
I will do what I can.

WHAT'S LEFT

Sometimes, happiness is all we have left.
We have squandered all our unhappiness, held on to it

So much and so long, had it for lunch, put it
On our faces, breathed it, talked it, given it to others:

Sadness, unhappiness, and all its other names, sadness—
One day we have used it all up. One day, it happens,

Just like that. We look around and we have
No shadow. It must be noon, so this is no proof.

We try frowning, try hard, realizing suddenly
We don't know how—we just always did,

So that trying to frown now is like trying to breathe—
We're too self-conscious. It's so obvious we're trying,

We try too hard. Of course it appears false,
A very bad job of acting. We frown that we cannot frown,

But even that look is curious and equally unconvincing,
Still second-rate and embarrassing, so that we stop.

It's a dark cloud that follows me, you think.
But the day is stormy. All the clouds are dark.

Your remark is unimpressive, and you are glad
You have not said it out loud. You are glad.

You are glad, but the feeling is strange.
You open the mail, expecting—of course—a paper cut.

It does not happen, even as you try to force it a little.
Your attempt is clumsy. Instead of a cut, the envelope,

Badly licked, comes open, just like that. It's bad news,
Of course, only the envelope has been misaddressed—

It is not your letter. There is the work of returning it now
Back to the box, but as you do so, reaching in,

You find the letter you had not seen before,
A letter that had somehow been pushed to the back.

You open it. It is not good news. But then again,
It is not bad news. Even better, you note, *it needs no reply.*

Dinner will have burned by now, you think. So there.
But you never turned on the stove. You will have to eat

Later, then, which is always upsetting. But of all things it is
The shift to daylight savings time today, and you gain an hour,

Or else the batteries have died and the clock is wrong,
Or else it turns out that you are hungrier than you thought

Later in an evening. And there are leftovers. They are the kind
Best eaten cold. And with your hands. There are no dirty dishes.

All of this, it lasts a day, a full day, a day you can find
No fault with. By bedtime, you are exhausted from trying,

Exhaustion propelling you straightway into sleep, into dream—
A pathway that has been eluding you for months. Exhaustion,

Not understanding, not knowing who looks back at you in the mirror:
It is happiness, all of this. A strange day. A strange day.

ABOUT THE AUTHOR

Alberto Ríos, born in Nogales, Arizona, is the author of ten books and chapbooks of poetry, including *The Theater of Night*, winner of the 2007 PEN/Beyond Margins Award, and *The Smallest Muscle in the Human Body*, a finalist for the National Book Award. He also has three collections of short stories, and a memoir about growing up on the border, *Capirotada*, which has just been voted the OneBookArizona 2009 selection. Ríos is the recipient of numerous other honors, including the Western Literature Association Distinguished Achievement Award, and his work is included in over 200 national and international literary anthologies, along with many public art installations. His work is regularly taught and translated, and has been adapted to dance and both classical and popular music.

Ríos is presently a Regents' Professor and the Katharine C. Turner Distinguished Chair in English at Arizona State University, where he has taught for twenty-seven years. Currently living in Chandler, Arizona, he has lived all over the state and was recently designated an Arizona Historymaker by the Arizona Historical League, a lifetime achievement award.

The Chinese character for poetry is made up of two parts: "word" and "temple." It also serves as pressmark for Copper Canyon Press.

Since 1972, Copper Canyon Press has fostered the work of emerging, established, and world-renowned poets for an expanding audience. The Press thrives with the generous patronage of readers, writers, booksellers, librarians, teachers, students, and funders—everyone who shares the belief that poetry is vital to language and living.

Major funding has been provided by:
Anonymous
Beroz Ferrell & The Point, LLC
Cynthia Hartwig and Tom Booster
Lannan Foundation
National Endowment for the Arts
Cynthia Lovelace Sears and Frank Buxton
Washington State Arts Commission

NATIONAL
ENDOWMENT
FOR THE ARTS

WASHINGTON STATE
ARTS COMMISSION

For information and catalogs:
COPPER CANYON PRESS
Post Office Box 271
Port Townsend, Washington 98368
360-385-4925
www.coppercanyonpress.org

The typefaces for this book are Cochin, designed by by Georges Peignot for Linotype, and New Caledonia, designed by William Addison Dwiggins. Book design and composition by Phil Kovacevich.

CPSIA information can be obtained
at www.ICGtesting.com
Printed in the USA
JSHW081417010523
41085JS00004B/5